THE G.I. SERIES

General Orders No. 3, 24 March 1858, also permitted the cocked hat or chapeau as optional wear for generals and field officers. The commanding colonel of the Eleventh Infantry, Erasmus Keyes, wears such a chapeau in lieu of the 1858-pattern
hat. He wears the double-breasted frock coat with seven buttons in each row as was regulation for field grade officers from
1851 until 1872. He has draped his crimson silk officer's sash 'scarf fashion', as did most officers of the day, rather than
correctly wrapping it around the waist twice and tying it behind the left hip. The trousers are sky blue, a color change that
was inaugurated in 1861, shortly after the Civil War commenced. *MJM*

THE G. I. SERIES

THE ILLUSTRATED HISTORY OF THE AMERICAN SOLDIER, HIS UNIFORM AND HIS EQUIPMENT

Fix Bayonets

The U.S. Infantry from the American Civil War to the Surrender of Japan

John P. Langellier

CHELSEA HOUSE PUBLISHERS

PHILADELPHIA

First Chelsea House hardback edition published 2000.

© Lionel Leventhal Limited, 1998
The moral right of the author has been asserted.

Library of Congress Cataloging-in-Publication Data
Langellier, J. Philip
Fix bayonets: the U.S. infantry from the American Civil War to the surrender of Japan / John P. Langellier.
    p. cm.— (The G.I. series)
Originally published: London: Greenhill Books; Mechanicsburg, PA: Stackpole Books, © 1998, in series: G.I. series; 14
Includes index.
Summary: A history of the United States infantry from the 1860s to 1945 with a focus on its uniforms and equipment.
ISBN 0-7910-5378-4 (hc)
1. United States. Army—Uniforms—History—19th century.   2. United States. Army—Uniforms—History—20th century.   3. United States. Army—Equipment—History—19th century.   4. United States. Army—Equipment—History—20th century.
[1. United States. Army—Uniforms—History.
2. United States. Army—Equipment—History.]
I. Title.   II. Series: G.I. series (Philadelphia, Pa.)
UD373.L35   1999
356'.1114'0973—dc21   99-13173
                                                         CIP

DEDICATION

This book is dedicated to friend and dedicated historian, Thomas Lindmier.

ACKNOWLEDGEMENTS AND ABBREVIATIONS

The author wishes to thank Christopher Anderson; LTC Leonid Kondratiuk National, Chief, Historical Services, National Guard Bureau; Dr. Michael J. McAfee; and the individuals or staffs of the institutions who are credited with the relevant illustrations as follows:

DB	Denis Bitterlich
FAM	Frontier Army Museum, Fort Leavenworth, KS
FLNHS	Fort Larned National Historic Site, Larned, KS
FSHM	Fort Sam Houston Museum, San Antonio, TX
GS	Glen Swanson
HB	Herb Peck
JG	Jerome Green
KSHS	Kansas State Historical Society, Topeka
LC	U.S. Library of Congress
MHS	Montana Historical Society, Helena, MT
MJM	Dr. Michael J. McAfee
NA	National Archives, Washington, DC
NAC	National Archives of Canada, Ottawa, Ontario
NPS	National Park Service, Golden Gate National Recreation Area
SC	Signal Corps, U.S. Army
SHSND	State Historical Society of North Dakota, Bismark, ND
SHSW	State Historical Society of Wisconsin, Madison, WI
UK	University of Kansas Libraries, Joseph Pennell Collection, Kansas Collection, Lawrence, KS
USA	USA Army, Presidio of San Francisco, CA
USAMHI	U.S. Army Military History Institute, Carlisle Barracks, PA
USAQM	U.S. Army Quartermaster Museum, Fort Lee, VA
WCC	Western Costume Company, North Hollywood, CA
WPM	West Point Museum, United States Military Academy
WSM	Wyoming State Museum, Cheyenne, WY

Designed and edited by DAG Publications Ltd
Designed by David Gibbons
Layout by Anthony A. Evans
Printed in Hong Kong

FIX BAYONETS

THE U.S. INFANTRY FROM THE AMERICAN CIVIL WAR TO THE SURRENDER OF JAPAN

In 1861, the year Abraham Lincoln took office as president, 183 of the 198 artillery, cavalry, and infantry companies of the United States Army were scattered at seventy-nine posts in the American West. In total, the republic's entire standing army consisted of between 13,000 and 16,000 men, including only ten infantry regiments. Serving across a vast nation, the American military was small in size and ill prepared for the coming strife that erupted when the attack on Fort Sumter, South Carolina tore the country asunder.

Soon after the opening salvos of the Civil War, the far-flung companies of foot soldiers had to be assembled and consolidated into regiments for the first time in memory. They would be led by officers who, for the most part, had previously commanded no more than a hundred or so men. Although many of these officers had fought in the Mexican War, that experience was more than a dozen years in the past.

Neither the North nor the South was in an immediate position to take up campaigning in earnest. Armies had to be created. To this end, Lincoln directed that thirty-nine regiments of infantry and one of cavalry be enlisted for three years service as volunteers. Soon thereafter, he called for an expansion of the Regulars, including nine more infantry regiments.

The War Department had given the matter of organization some thought even before Lincoln's additions to the Regular Army. In the past, American foot regiments were structured along the British model of ten companies each, with the regiment and battalion being synonymous. The new units, however, were to be patterned after the French, with three battalions to the regiment, each consisting of eight companies per battalion. In theory, two of the battalions could be ordered to the field while the third remained behind as a headquarters cadre for gathering and training recruits and replacements.

Thus two structures existed side by side, with the First to Tenth U.S. Infantry regiments being single battalion entities having a maximum strength of eighty-four enlisted men per company, while the Eleventh to Nineteenth U.S. Infantry regiments were to have three battalions with as many as ninety-seven rankers per company. Regardless of which organization was followed these numbers never were achieved because of the successful recruiting by volunteer units that took the lion's share of enlistees. In fact, by the end of 1861 only 11,000 of the 30,000 Regular infantrymen allotted were actually on the rolls. This continued to be the situation, thereby dictating that the third battalion of five of the new regiments (the Twelfth, Thirteenth, Fourteenth, Seventeenth, and Nineteenth) was never formed.

As the war continued the situation worsened. The Regulars obtained replacements for losses at a slower rate than the volunteers, thereby causing strengths to diminish further. The Seventh U.S. Infantry demonstrated an extreme case, in that by 1864 only seven officers and thirty-eight enlisted men remained in the unit, necessitating their consolidation into a single tiny company posted to guard duty.

What this meant was that volunteer infantrymen did most of the fighting by virtue of their sheer quantity. The large number of casualties sustained by the volunteers bore out this fact. In many respects they, along with the Regulars, fell victim to the deadly improvements in small arms that had been developed recently and wielded with savage impact during the Civil War. Unfortunately, tactics were not modified sufficiently to keep pace with advances in ordnance technology.

Not surprisingly, after 1865, when the fighting between the Union and Confederacy concluded, some military leaders sought a new means of deploying foot soldiers in battle. Major General Emory Upton, a sage Civil War veteran, became a key player in this effort. Soon after the war his tactics, which were much simpler and easier to learn than earlier versions, were adopted. Upton's drill, based upon evolutions of sets of fours, remained the standard for nearly a quarter century thereafter.

Not only was a new manual employed, but new breech-loading long arms also gradually replaced muzzle-loaders. A number of options were available. Eventually, a metallic cartridge .50 caliber Springfield with a flip up 'trapdoor' block was sent out from the U.S. Army's arsenal of that name. The basic design became the official weapon of American infantrymen, although by 1873 it was in the slightly smaller .45 caliber. This black powder weapon, like Upton's tactics, remained the bedrock for foot soldiers until the 1890s.

During this period most Springfields saw service across the Mississippi River where the final dramatic clashes with American Indians were being played out between the Mexican border and the boundary with Canada. Footsore 'walk-a-heaps' took to the field against Apaches, Lakotas, and other native peoples who often were more mobile and at times better armed than Uncle Sam's stalwart infantrymen. When not engaged in actual combat with a determined adversary, the infantry guarded military posts and lines of communication; helped build roads and forts; provided escorts to military and civilian travelers; and undertook a wide range of duties that were, at times, more monotonous than dangerous.

Once more these assignments were usually carried out from tiny one- and two-company posts sprinkled all over the huge expanse of the American West. And as before the Civil War, ten-company regiments were the norm. There were differences, however, since right after the war forty-five Regular Army infantry regiments were established, although by 1869 these were consolidated into twenty-five regiments, two of which were made up of black enlisted men.

Although more regiments existed than previously, actual strengths tended to be well under the figure authorized by Congress. In fact, by 1890, as the campaigns against American Indians approached an end, Companies I and K of each regiment were disbanded and the men dispersed to the remaining eight companies. In the process many small frontier posts were abandoned while several regiments were consolidated at the larger posts spared from closure.

During this period of reorganization the infantry was not in the best state of readiness, although it at least had a number of advantages over the foot soldiers of the past, including the School of Application for Infantry and Cavalry, established in 1881 at Fort Leavenworth, Kansas. Here, select junior officers gained experience in combined arms operations. Moreover, there was a new manual, *The Infantry Drill Regulations*, adopted in 1891, which reflected a heightened awareness of the importance of the squad and platoon in modern combat. A third improvement was a new smokeless powder .30 caliber rifle with a five-round capacity magazine that began to replace the old .45 caliber black powder single shot, from 1894. Consequently, this weapon (the Krag-Jörgensen) was in the hands of the infantry in time for its first overseas foray in half a century.

In 1898, the United States and Spain went to war over, initially, Spanish rule in Cuba. Unfortunately, most of the U.S. military leaders lacked the field experience to command a large army destined for foreign shores. Equipping the force of approximately 26,000 enlisted men, and training it for the fight ahead, was made even more difficult with the rapid expansion by reinforcements of another 125,000 volunteers, a number that soon escalated to 267,000 troops. As part of the process, the existing Regular infantry regiments also jumped from an average of fifty men to 106. Additionally, the two companies from each regiment that had been mothballed returned to the rolls and the short-lived three-battalion Civil War structure was adopted again for all Regular Army infantry regiments, thereby increasing the strength of these units to 1,300. These outfits would be joined by volunteers raised from the various states as well as ten regiments of infantry not connected with any specific area.

The force proved more than adequate for the task. Fighting concluded soon after hostilities began, leaving the United States a victorious, embryonic international power. In fact, the country now looked for possessions beyond its own shores to outlying territories in the Caribbean and Pacific – most notably Hawaii, the Philippines, Puerto Rico, and Panama, where the U.S. became involved in the construction of a major canal. In recognition of an increased mission for the military, during 1901 Congress authorized five more Regular infantry regiments, the Twenty-sixth to the Thirtieth, as well as providing for six more NCOs and raising the number of privates to 127 per company, when the president deemed it necessary to expand to this ceiling.

Besides additions to the ranks, a new bolt-action rifle replaced the Krag. The .30 caliber Springfield, like its predecessor, had a five-round magazine. This small arm boasted some of the most up-to-date technology of the era, and remained the combat weapon for U.S. infantrymen for nearly forty years.

A little over a decade after the M1903 Springfield's introduction, the table of organization for a U.S. infantry regiment was revised. This 1915 structure called for 959 officers and men in peacetime and 1,945 in time of war. By the next year the National Defense Act brought further increases with the size of the U.S. Army being raised from 100,000 to 175,000. This escalation included seven new infantry regi-

ments that were to be established with cadres from the existing units.

In 1917, when the Yanks entered World War I, twenty-seven more regiments were called up, bringing the total of Regular Army infantry to sixty-five regiments. These units would be incorporated into twenty divisions. Ultimately several adjustments were made in the formula for divisions, brigades, and regiments, for the most part to cope with the grueling demands of trench warfare. For instance, infantry regiments leapt from 2,002 to 3,720, and could have as many as fifteen companies, one of which was the machine gun company, an element of ever-increasing importance in breaking the stalemate on the Western Front. Besides automatic weapons, hand grenades and rifle grenades were added to the arsenal, usually with one expert in each of these specialties being included in every squad. Sometimes such specialists were staged in groups, a practice that existed as late as the Meuse–Argonne offensive of 1918.

World War I also necessitated small, dispersed unit tactics. Enhanced signal capabilities allowed better coordination of these scattered doughboys, while motor vehicles sometimes permitted more rapid troop movement, particularly for reinforcements from the rear, who could be rushed toward the front along with critical supplies.

After the Armistice in 1918, increased mechanization became a prime objective for troop transport. Within another two decades the emphasis shifted to even greater speed of deployment through the use of aircraft. Indeed, while military leaders gave greater emphasis to aviation, the foot soldier's lot was one of decline in the years between the two world wars. For instance, infantrymen had constituted nearly half of the U.S. Army's force, but by the 1930s this proportion dropped to just under twenty-five per cent. All these cutbacks meant elimination of twenty-seven regiments during the 1920s. In 1930, another five battalions were sacrificed to provide personnel for the expanding Army Air Corps.

This downward trend began to reverse by the mid-1930s, when Franklin Roosevelt's administration appropriated additional funds to add personnel to the Army as one means of recovery from the Depression. Growing tensions abroad also heightened the urgency to replenish the ranks. By 1939, 17,000 more infantrymen had been enlisted over the low point experienced just seven years earlier. Likewise, $1,000,000,000 was spent on restoring many of the inactivated regiments. This was followed in 1940 by the induction of forty national guard infantry regiments into the Federal service and another thirty-six by 1941, bringing the strength to nearly 380,000 infantrymen in 136 regiments, including eighteen armored infantry regiments and thirty-two battalions of armored infantry. Nearly half of the latter units were made up of light tanks. Eventually these numbers would increase dramatically as national guard units joined the equation to put the Americans on a wartime footing.

Nevertheless, the Chief of Infantry (a position created in 1920) pointed out that his branch constituted approximately twenty-five per cent of the U.S. Army while the German infantry constituted half of the entire Nazi establishment. The office of the chief did more than underscore the problems faced against a potential enemy's ground forces. For one thing, during the period between the two world wars this staff oversaw the development of the tank, both in terms of hardware and doctrine. Additionally, planners rearranged the table of organization, creating one for war and one for peace. This included the reduction of the number of platoons in a company from four to three, and by eliminating one rifle company per battalion to replace it with a machine gun company. While this consolidated the heavy machine guns in a manner that allowed the battalion commander to take direct control, the overall result was a lessening of firepower in the other companies.

This was offset somewhat by the addition of the Browning automatic rifle (BAR), a weapon used in limited form in World War I and improved thereafter, so that it was issued to one man in every squad for a brief period. Then, in 1942, the BAR was placed in a separate squad within the rifle platoon. In due course, the establishment of a weapons platoon (1939) added even more punch to a unit, whereby all the necessary special weapons except tanks and artillery were integrated for use.

While such innovations were being implemented, the United States Army likewise looked for an improved weapon for the individual rifleman as well. The result was the M1 Garand that began to phase out the Springfield bolt-action in the late 1930s. Widespread issue of this rifle, which had twice its predecessor's rate of fire, caused a drastic reduction of automatic weapons in a regiment. Ultimately this meant that, unlike the enemy, the G.I.'s firepower came from combining riflemen rather than from a crew-served weapon.

Besides this, the American infantry divisions had a company of light tanks to provide mobility and punch. Other vehicles were added, gradually increasing the speed of transport. However, the majority of U.S. infantrymen in World War II, like those of the past, went into combat on foot. From their first encounters after Pearl Harbor to the surrender of Imperial Japan's mighty war machine, these G.I.s fought a determined enemy with resolve, good marksmanship, and guts. And occasionally they came face to face with the foe, closing with fixed bayonets. In the end, such individual effort, replicated time and time again by millions of infantrymen, brought victory.

FOR FURTHER READING

Mahon, John K., and Danysh, Romana. *Infantry, Part I: Regular Army.* Army Linage Series. Washington, DC: Office of the Chief of Military History, 1972.

Sawicki, James A. *Infantry Regiments of the U.S. Army.* Dumfries: Wyvern Publications, 1981.

Thompson, Neil Baird. *Crazy Horse Called Them Walk-a-Heaps: The Story of the Foot Soldier in the Prairie Indian Wars.* St. Cloud: North Star Press, 1979.

Urwin, Gregory J.W. *The United States Infantry: An Illustrated History, 1775-1918.* London: Blandford Press, 1988.

Left: A sergeant major of infantry in the 1861 to 1872 regulation uniform for formal wear, including the M1840 NCO sword on the left and the scarlet worsted sash. *USAQM*

Right: The single-breasted overcoat with short cape was standard for foot troops as early as 1851 and remained regulation through the early 1870s. The cloth for the overcoat was sky blue kersey, as was the material for the trousers of 1861 and throughout the 1870s. *USAQM*

Left: The standard infantry enlisted field uniform consisting of the forage cap, four-button blouse, and light blue kersey trousers as worn from 1861 until the early 1870s. *USAQM*

Right: Company grade foot officers, such as the heavy artillery officer in the left foreground and the infantry officer standing next to him with folded arms, had a spiked helmet with chin chain for full dress that was combined with the double-breasted 1880-pattern coat bearing seven officers' buttons in each row (these buttons were gilt with a spread eagle that had a shield on the chest with a superimposed 'I' for 'infantry' in the center). Field grade infantry officers (from major to colonel) and regimental adjutants were to have plumed helmets, like the colonel seated in the foreground. *GS*

Left: During the Spanish American War, although a new khaki uniform was among several additions to the combat outfit, the old 1883-pattern field shirt and 1884-pattern blue trousers, with 1½-inch white stripes on the outer seams for infantry officers, remained a common field uniformcombined along with either the 1889 or 1899-pattern drab campaign hat.

Below: In 1884, the long-standing light blue facings for infantry were changed to white. A new collar was also adopted with a slightly altered tail flashing as well for the dress enlisted coat in that year, as were gold lace chevrons for non-commissioned officers. In 1895, a new forage cap replaced the former 'kepi' style as seen on the first sergeant in his garrison uniform in the center of this illustration by H. A. Ogden. The officer's version of the cap can be seen on the lieutenant holding his M1860 staff and field sword, second from right, who appears in the 1895-pattern officer's jacket. The khaki uniform, prescribed in 1898 after the out-break of the war with Spain, is also evident. It was to have white shoulder loops for Regular Army infantrymen, despite the incorrect depiction by the artist of blue loops on the officer to the far right. *WCC*

Infantry Private	Infantry Musician	Infantry Corporal	Infantry Line Officer (Lieut.)	Infantry Field Officer (Colonel)	Infantry First Sergeant Undress or Fatigue	Infantry Private, Campaign (Khaki)	Infantry Private Regular Campaign Uniform	Infantry Line Officer (First Lieutenant) Fatigue or Undress	Infantry Line Officer (Rank not shown) Campaign (Khaki)

At the end of 1902, new regulations made sweeping changes in the uniform of the U.S. Army, including the adoption of a single-breasted infantry enlisted dress coat with stand collar which was piped in sky blue, along with a welt of matching piping running horizontally above the cuffs. A light blue breast cord and a band with light blue stripes were other features of the full dress uniform, both being removable to convert the kit into 'dress.' *WCC*

In 1883, a medium brown color canvas overcoat with blanket lining was adopted as an outer garment for extreme cold. This item was usually combined with fur gauntlets and a cap with flaps, and continued to be issued into the early twentieth century. In 1902, a new olive drab (OD) wool overcoat was adopted, however, and earlier patterns were gradually phased out. The OD version could be worn with white Berlin gloves, canvas leggings, and service cap for garrison, as the corporal standing in the center of this illustration has done; or with Arctic overshoes and canvas blanket lined cap, as the seated sergeant wears; or with fur mittens, cowl, and cap, as the private in the background depicts. There was also a 1902-pattern olive drab ulster overcoat for officers on which rank was depicted by flat black mohair soutache braid ⅛-inch in width at the cuffs. A plain sleeve was designated for second lieutenants, a single braid for first lieutenants, two braids for captains, and so forth up to five braids for a colonel. *WCC*

Left: In 1911 the distinction of having seven buttons in each row for the double-breasted full dress uniform coat of company grade officers (second lieutenants to captains) and nine buttons in each row for field grade officers (majors to colonels) was discontinued. In that year, all officers were to have nine buttons in each row, like this first lieutenant of the Seventeenth U.S. Infantry. By 1912, the full dress cap with sky blue band edged by gold wire lace was also to do double duty as the dress cap. Here was a difference for company grade officers who had plain black visors while field grade officers were to have gold embroidered 'scrambled eggs' on their visors. *DB*

Above: This detail of a painting of World War I 'doughboys' by Frank E. Schoonover, 1919, depicts the field kit with the heavy wool olive drab overcoat, overseas cap, and wrapped puttees. The latter two items were adapted from the Allies by the Yanks, after they arrived in Europe in 1917. *Collection Delaware National Guard. Photography by John R. Schoonover.*

Below: A World War II technical sergeant identified by his chevrons with three stripes points up and two 'rockers'

below, looks through his field glasses. He wears the M1 helmet and herringbone twill (HBT) olive drab shade No. 7 shirt, adopted in 1943 as part of the two-piece jungle and desert combat outfit. *SC*

Below: Scrambling over the side on ropes to board their rubber landing raft, these infantrymen have rolled up the legs of their HBT trousers as well as removed their boots, socks, and leggings to keep these items from being soaked. Their M26 life preservers are evident around their waists. *SC*

Below: A World War II combat infantryman in his M1943 field jacket loads a three-pocket grenade carrier with fragmentation grenades. *SC*

Above: A staff sergeant of the 10th Mountain Division stands tall in the cotton khaki shirt, trousers, and 'overseas' cap, as often worn in garrison. He proudly displays the blue-backed Combat Infantryman's Badge with silver rifle and wreath on the chest above his left pocket indicating his status as a veteran of an infantry regiment or battalion that has seen action against the enemy. *SC*

Left: General Orders No. 3, 24 March 1858, ushered in dark blue trousers with ⅛-inch sky blue welts for infantry officers, as seen here for Captain Nathaniel Lyon at the outset of the Civil War. Lyon wears the single-breasted nine-button dark blue wool frock of company grade officers with the 1851-pattern gold epaulets. He holds the 1858-pattern officer's hat which, for the infantry, bore a gold embroidered hunting horn device on the front. *USAMHI*

Right: Second Lieutenant John K. Clary, Fourteenth U.S. Infantry, also wears the sky blue trousers with ⅛-inch dark blue welt for infantry officers, but has donned a chasseur type low-crowned forage cap for his headgear in the field as well as shoulder straps instead of epaulets. The strap centers were medium or light blue, and plain for second lieutenants. *USAMHI*

Above: Major H.B. Clitz, Twelfth U.S. Infantry, has turned back the collar of his double-breasted field grade officer's frock coat to form lapels. He also wears shoulder straps which would have displayed a gold oak leaf at each end of the blue field, and a chasseur style dark blue wool forage cap with gold embroidered infantry officer's device bearing a silver embroidered regimental numeral in the crook of the horn. *USAMHI*

Right: The regulation 1858-pattern hat was not popular among the rank and file. Originally, it was to be worn with the brim pinned up on the left side, until 1872 when this was changed to the right side for foot troops, as had been the case with cavalry prior to that time. This private from Company C, Seventeenth U.S. Infantry, follows those regulations for the dress uniform of the 1861–1872 period, including brass shoulder scales. *MJM*

Above: Bandsmen of the 107th Infantry
Regiment, U.S. Colored Troops, wear the
nine-button 1858-pattern enlisted infantry frock
coat without the traditional blue worsted tape
ornamentation on the chest called for by regulations. All are wearing the forage cap that
became closely associated with the Civil War
Union soldier. *LC*

Right: Regimental bandsmen, on the other hand,
often wore other types of accessories or uniforms that varied from the standard pattern
because regulations allowed wide latitude in
this instance. For example, trefoils and special
two-tone leg stripes are seen in the case of
bandsman Edwin Waterman. *MJM*

Above: The pattern of trousers remained the same from 1861 to 1876. Dark blue stripes formed part of the rank indication, this being an example prescribed for sergeants with 1½-inch worsted stripes. In turn, corporals were to have ½-inch worsted dark blue stripes, and privates none. Furthermore, sergeants were to have three stripes worn 'points down' on their coats and blouses of sky blue worsted to indicate their rank, and corporals two. This individual has the M1855 rifleman's belt and sword bayonet. *MJM*

Top right: NCOs with the regimental staff, such as this sergeant major, had sky blue silk chevrons. Instead of wearing the issue brass hunting horn, this Civil War era officer has procured an embroidered pattern for his forage cap. *MJM*

Right: These three Civil War Union infantrymen have all added waterproof covers to their forage caps. *MJM*

Right: Service chevrons, worn diagonally above the cuff piping or trim on the frock coat, were another type of chevron authorized for Regular Army infantrymen during the Civil War. This private had served two enlistments when this photograph was taken. The color of the worsted chevron coincided with the branch in which the individual served, such as sky blue for infantry, yellow for engineers and cavalry, and so forth. *MJM*

Left: Adopted in the late 1850s, both the four-button sack coat and forage cap remained in use until the early 1870s as part of the fatigue and field uniform. Insignia on the cap varied from unit to unit until standardized in the 1870s. *MJM*

Right: A single-breasted sky blue kersey overcoat with short cape was the cold weather issue of the Union infantry foot soldier. *MJM*

Below: In this c.1870 image, the Fifth U.S. Infantry band at Fort Leavenworth, Kansas, stands on the parade ground in their custom-made uniforms. In contrast to these musicians, on the far left of the photograph, the regiment's sergeant major appears with his left hand on his belt in the 1861 to 1872 pattern regulation infantry dress. *FAM*

Above: A group of privates and NCOs from the Eighteenth U.S. Infantry appear in the immediate post-Civil War uniform consisting of sky blue kersey trousers and dark blue 1858-pattern enlisted coat, piped in sky blue. A few of the men, such as the sergeant in the back row with the goatee, has obtained a lower crowned chasseur forage cap rather then the higher crowned regulation version. *FLNHS*

Right: On the right with his trapdoor rifle at the ready, this private of the Twentieth U.S. Infantry has fixed his bayonet, which he has removed from an atypical frog-mounted scabbard. This picture, taken in late 1872 or early 1873, indicates the transition in weapons, accoutrements and uniforms that occurred in the years after the Civil War. For instance, while the bayonet-wielding foot soldier wears the old four-button sack coat and floppy 'bummer's' cap, the private standing on the left has an 1872-pattern low-crowned forage cap. He also wears the 1872-pattern pleated blouse, a garment which took its inspiration from British civilian hunting jackets. This blouse was produced for fatigue and campaign wear, although it proved unpopular with the rank and file. Sky blue worsted cord trimmed the collar, yoke, and cuffs, and nine brass 1854-pattern general service buttons appeared in a single row on the front. *NAC, Negative Number C8716*

Left: Sky blue mohair trim and a white pompom were among the distinguishing features of the 1872-pattern infantry enlisted cap which remained in use until replaced by a spiked helmet for dress occasions in 1881. From 1872 to 1875 a hunting horn was affixed to the front of the cap. Thereafter, regulations called for crossed rifles, the company letter, and regimental numeral in brass to appear on the cap while the regimental numeral was to be affixed to both sides of the collar facings. A dark blue wool 1872-pattern dress coat trimmed with light blue facings and piping was the other basic component for the infantryman on formal occasions according to the 1872 regulations. The old model cartridge box supported by an over-the-shoulder strap was replaced while this new uniform was being produced. *USAQM*

Right: Musicians in the regimental band, however, could deviate from regulations, as had long been the custom. For instance, this infantry bandsman at Fort Leavenworth in the 1870s has a triple row of buttons on his coat which appears to be faced in white rather than light blue. He also sports cords, worsted epaulets, a white leg stripe (probably piped in scarlet), and cock feathers on his dress cap. *FAM*

Right: In 1872, infantry musicians serving with companies were to have the same dress coat as all other enlisted men except that the chest of the coat was ornamented with 'herring-bones' that emanated from the buttons, in the same shade of blue as the coat facings. The brass regimental numerals were affixed to the facings on the collar by brass wires. *GS*

Opposite, top left: In 1875, crossed rifles replaced the traditional hunting horn as the insignia for infantry, as seen here for this private. The company letter appeared in the lower angle while the regimental number was placed in the upper angle of the insignia. The regimental number was also worn on the collar until 1884. *MJM*

Opposite, top right: The 1872-pattern infantry officer's dress uniform consisted of a cap with flat gold braid trim, a gold embroidered hunting horn, and white cock feathers. Shoulder knots bore silver embroidered regimental numbers in the center of pads covered in light or medium blue facing material. Two flat gold lace vertical bars appeared at the cuff

for company grade officers (second lieutenants as seen here, to captains) and three lace bars were called for in the case of field grade infantry officers (majors to colonels). Trouser stripes of dark blue 1½-inch facing material appeared on the outer seams for all infantry officers, replacing the ⅛-inch welt of the past. *GS*

Below: For field and garrison wear, officers had a five-button blouse with black mohair braid ornamentation. Shoulder straps indicated rank, as seen here for this second lieutenant of the Thirteenth U.S. Infantry. The 1872-pattern forage cap for infantry officers bore an embroidered gold hunting horn with silver regimental number. *GS*

Left: A company of the Sixteenth U.S. Infantry at Fort Riley, Kansas, c.1880, have mounted trowel bayonets on their .45 caliber Springfield rifles. These were examples of experimental equipment items issued to some units in the post-Civil War era. *KSHS*

Right: The 1874-pattern blouse for infantrymen was piped in light blue cord on the cuffs and collar and had five buttons down the front. This streamlined field and garrison jacket was used side by side with the 1872-pattern pleated blouse for several years. While, typically, only one small enlisted button appeared at the outer edge of the cuff piping, some men had three buttons sewn to their cuffs, as is the case with the seated infantry corporal (so indicated by what appears to be the correct ½-inch dark blue trouser stripe). *MJM*

Below: Men of the Fifth U.S. Infantry stand outside their Sibley tents in Montana Territory, 1878. Many appear to be wearing 1874-pattern shirts, and most have 1876-pattern trousers. One man (near the center, next to the bugler, and with his hands clasped) even wears either the 1872-pattern dress coat (an unlikely garment for campaign) or possibly a converted 1858-pattern enlisted frock coat. Headgear varies from 1872-pattern forage caps to black 1876-pattern campaign hats and more practical light-colored civilian slouch hats. *NA*

Left: In 1881 a spiked helmet replaced the infantry cap with pompom. Otherwise the uniform remained relatively unchanged, save the introduction of new pattern trousers in 1876. This sergeant of the Twentieth U.S. Infantry appears in the regulation dress for the 1881–84 period, complete with dark blue 1-inch leg stripes on his trousers. *FAM*

Below: Three second lieutenants attending the School of Infantry and Cavalry Application at Fort Leavenworth, Kansas, wear the 1881-pattern company grade infantry officer's dress helmet with chin chain and the 1880-pattern dress coat. Knots remained medium to dark blue with the regimental numeral. The belts were gold lace with three horizontal medium to dark blue stripes. *FAM*

Left: 1884 saw the removal of piping from the cuffs and collar of the five-button enlisted blouse. This was also the last year that service stripes were worn on the blouse. This sergeant, from either the Twenty-fourth or Twenty-fifth U.S. Infantry, appears in the blouse of that period with custom chevrons made of separately applied facing stripes. He also has, on the collar of his jacket, the marks-manship devices adopted in the late 1870s. *HP*

Opposite page, left: 1884 also marked the adoption of gold lace chevrons, in this case general service stripes worn above the cuffs to indicate completion of a five-year period of enlist-ment, replacing the pat-tern made from facing material for use on dress coats. In the same year, collar numerals were dis-continued and all infantry facings were changed from sky blue to white, as shown on this c.1885 portrait of Private Carter Huse of the Twenty-fifth U.S. Infantry. *SHSND*

Opposite page, right: Company musicians con-tinued the herring-bone pattern adopted in 1872 but now the material was white instead of sky blue. Trousers bore double white $\frac{1}{2}$-inch stripes for musicians while corpo-rals wore a single $\frac{1}{2}$-inch stripe and sergeants a single 1-inch stripe on the outer seams of their trousers, new patterns of which were adopted in 1884 and again in 1885. The sword is the M1840 musician's pattern. *GS*

Above: From 1881 to 1902, regulations called for company grade infantry officers to have double-breasted coats with seven buttons in each row and field grade officers to have nine buttons in each row. The former were to have spiked helmets while the latter, along with regimental adjutants, were to have plumed helmets with white yak or buffalo plumes as seen here in this group portrait taken of Seventeenth U.S. Infantry officers around 1884, just before the branch facing color changed from blue to white. The officers standing on each end of the front row are not infantrymen, but belong to the Seventh U.S. Cavalry. *GS*

Left: From 1884 to 1903, company grade infantry officers' dress uniforms had white facings on the pad of the knots and a white 1½-inch leg stripe down the outer seams of the trousers. The gold lace belt exhibited three horizontal white stripes as well. The sword is the M1860 staff and field pattern.

Left: In 1875, crossed rifles replaced the hunting horn for infantry officers and enlisted men. For the latter, gold embroidered crossed rifles were to be surmounted by a silver embroidered regimental number, as here for the Twenty-fourth U.S. Infantry. A gold cap cord was adopted for officers' forage caps by General Order No. 102, 26 December 1883, sanctioning an item previously worn unofficially in lieu of the regulation leather strap. From 1884, shoulder straps were to have white backgrounds. In 1875, the mohair trim was deleted from officers' sack coats. *FAM*

Right: From 1881, a plumed helmet with white yak or buffalo hair became the dress headgear of infantry field grade officers and regimental adjutants, in addition to the spiked helmet. The latter also had aiguillettes suspended from their right shoulder, attached under the knot, to further indicate their position, as the Sixth U.S. Infantry second lieutenant does in this c.1885 image. *FAM*

Left: After 1884, piping was also to be removed from the enlisted blouse, which became more tailored than earlier patterns. Additionally, trousers began to have more of a flare at the cuffs, especially the type adopted in the mid-1880s. Even then, older accoutrements, such as components of the short-lived infantry brace system belt with its distinctive buckle, were issued in tandem with later uniforms, as seen here in the case of Private George Whitaker, First U.S. Infantry, Company C, in late 1880s. *JG*

Opposite page, top left: Beginning in the 1870s, buffalo overcoats became available for limited issue, as worn by this private of Company A, Twenty-fifth U.S. Infantry in the 1880s. *HP*

Opposite page, top right: A trio of infantry enlisted men in this mid-1880s studio portrait have replaced their 1872-pattern forage caps with rakish civilian 'porkpie' hats. While the headgear was not regulation, vests and cravats were permitted by this period as well, but had to be bought by the soldier rather than being issue items. Because a private was paid only $13 per month, additional clothing items were probably viewed as an extravagance. *WSM*

Opposite page, bottom: In 1880, cork summer helmets covered with white cloth were permitted for all officers, like the one worn by this Twentieth U.S. Infantry officer posted at Fort Keogh, Montana. *NA*

Left: Three proud privates of the Sixth U.S. Infantry, Company D, wear the new 1895-pattern forage cap with one-piece cap insignia affixed with a screw-back post, rather than separately applied rifles, regimental number, and company letter fastened with flimsy brass wires. Note the 'pinked' white trim on the interior of blouse worn by the man standing in the background. While not regulation, such privately tailored blouses were not uncommon by the 1890s, and starched detachable linen shirt collars, either privately purchased or of the 1887-pattern issue, were also typical of the period. *FAM*

Opposite page, top: The enlisted 1880-pattern summer helmet was covered in white canvas. White trousers were permitted in southern latitudes, such as at Fort Sam Houston, Texas, where this formation took place around 1895. These trousers had been sanctioned nearly two decades before this photograph was taken. *FSHM*

Opposite page, bottom: Officers of the Twenty-fifth U.S. Infantry appear in the new 1892-pattern blouse with stand collar and black mohair accents, including trefoils on the chest and 'Austrian' knots on the lower sleeve similar to those that had adorned the 1872-pattern officer's blouse. A silver metal regimental numeral was to be worn on each side of the collar. *NA*

Right: The 1895-pattern enlisted forage cap could also be combined with the light blue overcoat which, from 1879, was to have a dark blue lined cape. Just three years earlier, dark blue chevrons with stripes in white silk chain stitching were prescribed for infantry NCOs' overcoats, to ensure that the rank stood out clearly against the light cloth. From 1883, chevrons were worn below the overcoat elbows, two inches above the cuff, so that they were not covered by the cape. *NA*

Opposite page, top: In 1895, the leather belt with rectangular brass buckle was dispensed with, even for full dress. Blue canvas Mill's cartridge belts were to be worn in a rather incongruous mixture for troops armed with the Krag rifle. *USA*

Opposite page, bottom: Towards the end of the nineteenth century, weapons and uniforms were not the only areas of change for the infantry. In a quest for heightened mobility, stalwart volunteers from the Twenty-fifth U.S. Infantry Regiment experimented with bicycles as a military vehicle. They are seen here in Montana in 1896 going over rugged terrain in Yellowstone National Park, wearing 1889-pattern campaign hats, 1883-pattern dark blue wool shirts, and 1885-pattern medium blue kersey trousers. *Haynes Foundation Collection, MHS*

Above: An infantry officer wears the stand collar mohair blouse adopted in 1895, which continued to be used into the twentieth century. The block style 'U.S.' insignia and crossed rifles with regimental numbers were to be positioned on the collar. These could be gilt metal or embroidered in gold. This jacket could be worn with the 1895-pattern officer's forage cap depicted on the man's lap, or the campaign hat. *USAMHI*

Left: When the weather cooled, a handsome dark blue cape with light blue lining and black velvet collar could be worn over the 1895-pattern officer's jacket or the overcoat. White facing was substituted in the late 1890s through the early twentieth century. *NA*

Left: The 1884-pattern surtout in dark blue wool could serve as an overcoat when the temperature dropped. Four black mohair frogs closed the front across the chest, and an optional hood was available for more protection than the forage cap afforded. *NA*

Opposite page, top: In the late 1880s, brown canvas leggings gradually began to be adopted to protect the lower legs of the foot soldier. These practical accessories created a multi-toned look when worn with the light blue kersey trousers and dark blue wool blouse, as depicted by this company on the eve of the Spanish American War. *WSM*

Opposite page, bottom: Soon after the United States went to war with Spain in 1898, a khaki uniform was adopted for the field. Infantry first lieutenants to lieutenant colonels wore their rank and the U.S. coat of arms on the white shoulder loops of their 1898-pattern khaki blouses, and the crossed rifles with regimental number on their collars. Colonels wore the coat of arms on the collar along with the infantry insignia, and only their eagles on the white shoulder loops, while second lieutenants, as seen here, had only the coat of arms on the loops, there being no insignia of rank at the time for these junior officers. *FAM*

Opposite page: In 1898, a dark blue serge blouse was provided as an option for officers' field wear. The shoulder straps authorized for the 1895-pattern officer's blouse were to be used, but in most other respects this garment resembled the khaki jacket in cut, including four exterior pockets, and metallic collar insignia. *FAM*

Right: The white, 1895-pattern officer's blouse had no official provision for shoulder straps to indicate rank or collar insignia. Even the forage cap had no coat of arms, and the chin strap cord was originally to be of white silk, which was practically invisible. *NA*

Below: Khaki uniforms, white uniforms, and blue wool uniform items remaining from earlier times, such as the 1883-pattern shirt to the 1895-pattern officer's blouse, were worn side by side during the late 1890s, as shown by this group of officers and enlisted men in the Philippines. Such a lack of uniformity was common among regulars and volunteers alike. The officers in the white 1895-pattern caps have added coats of arms to the front. They have also all added shoulder straps to their 1895-pattern white jackets, despite a lack of official sanction. Not until 1901 were provisions made to indicate rank for the white officer's blouse. *USA*

Left: This infantry private wears the enlisted version of the khaki jacket with stand collar and white shoulder loops of the type issued on a relatively limited basis in 1898. He also wears khaki trousers. *USA*

Below: By 1899, specifications for enlisted khaki blouses called for a roll collar, as seen here for this corporal who wears white Berlin gloves, evidently in readiness for an inspection or guard mount. *USA*

Left: While the khaki uniform was more suitable for campaign wear in the Spanish American War, most troops did not receive the new uniform before shipping overseas. Instead, dark blue wool 1883-pattern shirts and light blue kersey 1884-pattern or 1885-pattern trousers were worn with the 1889-pattern campaign hat, as these two infantry privates illustrate. *USAMHI*

Right: The 1883-pattern shirt was combined with khaki trousers in several instances, particularly late in the century. These trousers had belt loops, unlike the kersey versions. Another improvement was the addition of approximately 1-inch-diameter fine brass screen vents to the sides of crown of the new 1899-pattern campaign hat. *JG*

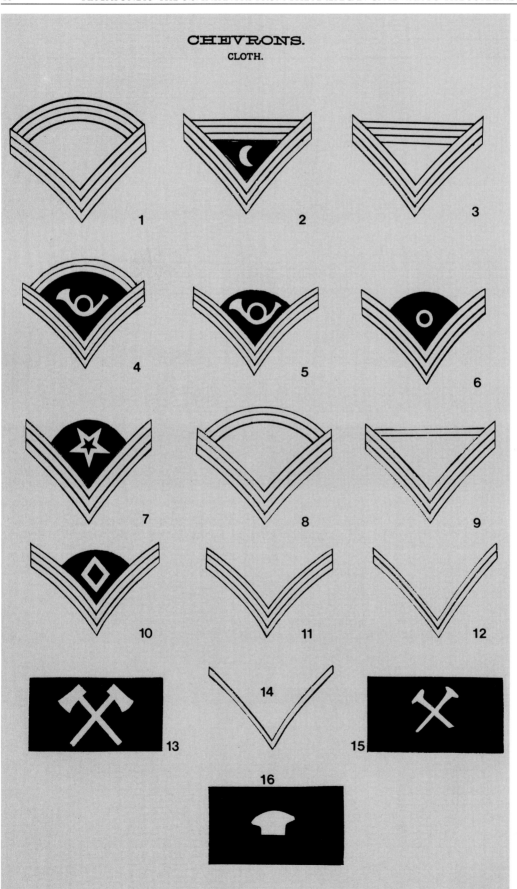

CHEVRONS.
CLOTH.

Left: From 1884, infantry chevrons for the five-button blouse were made of white facing material with black silk chain stitching to create stripes. The backgrounds for insets were of blue wool to match the blouse, as were the large backgrounds for brassards. There were versions made of duck for the khaki uniform as well, and in this case the backgrounds were of the same khaki material as the jackets. The ranks were as follows (dates in parentheses indicate year of adoption for the white chevrons): **1** sergeant major (1884, retitled regimental sergeant major 1899); **2** regimental commissary sergeant (1899); **3** quartermaster sergeant (1884, retitled regimental quartermaster sergeant 1899); **4** chief musician (1899); **5** principal musician (1884); **6** regimental color sergeant (1884, retitled regimental and battalion color sergeant 1885); **7** regimental color sergeant (1901); **8** battalion sergeant major (1899); **9** company quartermaster sergeant (1898); **10** first sergeant (1884); **11** sergeant (1884); **12** corporal (1884); **13** pioneer (1884); **14** lance corporal (1891); **15** artificer (1899); **16** cook (1898).

Right: In 1901, loops were added to the 1895-pattern white officer's jacket, upon which insignia of rank and a gilt metal arms of the United States could be placed for all officers below the rank of colonel (except second lieutenants who were to have only the arms of the United States), while the collar was to bear pin-backed crossed rifles and regimental number. This arrangement followed the one prescribed for the 1898-pattern khaki officer's blouse. *NA*

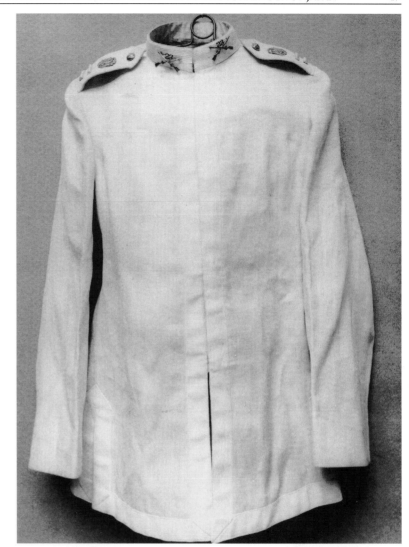

Below: At the end of 1902, a major uniform change was promulgated with numerous new patterns, although a number of previously issued items remained in service, such as the 1895-pattern forage cap and all the other nineteenth-century items still in use by men of Company G, Twenty-fifth U.S. Infantry in a picture taken about 1903. Only the small chevrons worn 'points up' are of the new 1902-pattern. *FSHM*

Left: The new 1902-pattern cap had a detachable band with a pair of light blue stripes of facing material sewn on a blue wool background. This was supposed to be removed to convert the headpiece into the dress cap from full dress, although this private of Twenty-fifth Infantry, Company I, ignored this requirement when he went to the photographer. He also continues to wear the nineteenth-century enlisted five-button blouse, but has added the new 1902-pattern 'U.S.' brass insignia to his collar, partly in keeping with the new arrangement for the enlisted uniforms adopted in 1902. *HP*

Right: The 1902-pattern regulation full dress uniform, as worn here by Private Arthur Wooland of Company M, Eighteenth U.S. Infantry, included a dark blue coat with six buttons. The shoulder loops, collar, and cuffs were trimmed in light blue mohair piping for infantry enlisted men. The collar was to bear brass regimental insignia on each side (crossed rifles with regimental number and the company letter) and a pair of 'U.S.' devices. A similar crossed rifles insignia was to be worn on the hat, kept in place by a screwpost fastener, while the collar insignia were to be pin-backs. A worsted light blue breast cord formed another part of the full dress. *FAM*

Above: Bandsmen could wear the same uniform as the other ranks for dress and full dress according to the 1902 regulations, but for their insignia they exchanged crossed rifles for a lyre, in this case surrounded by a wreath on the caps. They often continued to display the double ½-inch stripes of white facing material on their trousers, as do the two men seated in the right front of the photograph, in contrast to the two corporals on the left who have the ½-inch leg stripes associated with their rank. From 1902 to 1903, leg stripes for infantry were to be light blue, as were chevrons from 1903 to 1917; the full dress, dress chevrons and leg stripes were to be white. The chief musician of this band, of the Sixth U.S. Infantry, has a 1902-pattern officer's dress jacket and collar and a modified 1902-officer's cap with embroidered lyre and wreath instead of the U.S. coat of arms All wear light blue kersey trousers. They have removed their hat bands and breast cords to convert the full dress uniform to the dress uniform. *FAM*

Left: As in the past, regimental bands continued to enjoy latitude in their uniform design: this musician of the Thirteenth U.S. Infantry wears a coat which is a cross between the 1902-pattern enlisted dress and the 1902-pattern officer's dress with mohair braid. The chest ornamentation of black mohair harkens back to the old 1892-pattern officer's blouse. The collar brass was typical for bands, and the shooting medals (expert rifleman second from right and U.S. Army rifle competition in the middle), as well as medals for the Spanish Campaign (a castle for Cuba) and the Philippine Campaign (with a palm tree), the latter items being adopted in 1905. *FAM*

Olive drab (OD) was another innovation of the 1902 uniform changes, including a new service dress of wool for enlisted men with the jacket cut somewhat similar to the 1899-pattern enlisted blouse but with OD shoulder loops permanently affixed, rather than detachable ones in white. The buttons and collar insignia were dull bronze. Breeches, even for dismounted troops, also became part of the field and campaign uniform with this outfit, while new OD leggings were also adopted. Blue hat cords were worn on the 1902-pattern drab campaign hat with bronze company letters and regimental numbers attached to the front of the crown. Shorter leggings than the nineteenth-century patterns were issued with the new uniform; these approximated the shade of the breeches rather than being medium brown. *FAM*

Above: A detail of the collar insignia for infantry officers prescribed in 1902 is worn here by Captain H. Reeve, Third U.S. Infantry. The following year, the dull bronze coat of arms was replaced by a 'U.S.' The campaign hat varies from the issue item in that it has two small grommets in the crown rather than the regulation five-pointed star perforation. Officers' hat cords were black and gold intermixed for lieutenants to colonels, regardless of the branch. *NA*

Below: The regulation enlisted version of the 1902-pattern drab fur felt campaign hat had a five-pointed star on either side of the crown, and a ribbon with bow on the left side. The edge of the brim was turned up and sewn back on to itself, along with eyelets, one on each side, for a hat strap or cord to be inserted, both as a means of keeping the headgear on and as another way to keep the light blue infantry enlisted hat cord in place. *SHSW*

Above: The olive drab wool officer's service dress prescribed by the new 1902 regulations was of finer quality material than the issue for enlisted personnel. A new M1902 saber was to be used with this outfit, and boots rather than leggings were permitted for officers. Russet leather, such as the saber belt, was another of the 1902 departures, in that black had previously been the color for field leather. Footwear was to change to this color as well for the service uniform, thereby ushering in the era of the 'Brown Shoe' army. *FAM*

Left: Lieutenant F.L. Simpson, Eighth U.S. Infantry, in the 1902-pattern officer's dress coat with the arms of the United States insignia in gilt, which would be replaced the following year by gilt 'U.S.' devices. *NA*

Right: The infantry officer's full dress uniform consisted of a full dress coat with light blue collar edged in gold wire lace. Sleeve ornaments on this double-breasted garment indicated rank and branch. In the case of the infantry officer on the right, the sleeve is blank except for a band of gold wire lace, indicating that he is a second lieutenant, while the small shield denotes that he has been appointed as an aide de camp, as does the detachable gold aiguillette suspended from his right shoulder knot. In 1903, trouser stripes were changed to white from light blue, as depicted here. The band on the cap and the collar remained light blue, however. *FAM*

Above: The M1907 infantry equipment featured an OD belt with reinforced pocket bottoms to hold two five-round clips for the M1905 Springfield rifle. The belt was also used to attach the M1905 bayonet in its leather and canvas scabbard, the M1900 canteen from the M1904 web sling, the Hoff first-aid packet, and the M1903 haversack, all held up by suspenders. Most elements of this rig are evident in the case of the soldier in the right foreground. Both heavy artillery and infantry troops were issued this equipment. Also note the 1911-pattern 'Montana peak' campaign hats, with which infantrymen were to wear light blue worsted hat cords that terminated in acorns. *GS*

Left: Corporal C. Tucker Beckett, Sixteenth U.S. Infantry, wore his 1902-pattern full dress uniform, seen here without the breast cord, for the last time when he posed for a portrait at El Paso, Texas, in February 1916. He was to put aside this formal outfit with its dark blue coat piped in light blue with white chevrons, service stripes, and leg stripes on the light blue trousers (according to regulations assigning these colors in 1903) to don olive drab for the expedition with Brigadier General John J. Pershing into Mexico. A sharpshooters' device appears on the corporal's left breast. *NA*

Above: Men of Company G, Sixteenth U.S. Infantry serving in the 1916 Punitive Expedition, stand inspection in the M1910 infantry equipment and their OD wool service coats with 'Montana peaks.' *NA*

Right: Private Earl Avery, Company A, Twenty-fifth U.S. Infantry was photographed at Fort Riley, Kansas, in the 1911-pattern olive drab service coat (not actually issued until 1912) with the stand collar that was to bear circular disks in lieu of crossed rifles as insignia on the collar. The bronze disks were first proposed in 1907, but were not adopted until 1910, after several delays. These had screw-backs and measured one inch in diameter. Originally, the one on the left side was to bear crossed rifles with the regimental numeral above and company letter below, where applicable, while the one on the right was to display a 'U.S.' device. The hat cord continued to be light blue for the 1911-pattern campaign hat. In this photogtraph Avery also wears Expert Rifleman and Expert Pistol marksmanship awards. *UK*

Left: The 1911-pattern shirt often was used in lieu of the service coat during the Punitive Expedition. As of 30 December 1916, the bronze disk insignia could be placed on the shirt as well, although First Sergeant Blood, Company C, Sixteenth Infantry, in this photograph at El Valle, Mexico, July 1916, has elected not to do so. His olive drab chevrons with olive drab backing, as adopted on 31 December 1907, are evident, however. Prior to that the chevrons were sky blue on olive drab or khaki backgrounds depending upon the material color of the coat itself. *NA*

Opposite page, top: On duty during the 1916 Punitive Expedition, a crew of Sixteenth U.S. Infantry soldiers in 1911-pattern shirts and breeches man a Benét-Mercie M1909 .30 caliber 'automatic machine rifle,' a French-designed light machine gun manufactured in limited quantities by Colt and the Springfield Arsenal for U.S. Army use. *NA*

Below: A pair of M1905 Springfield rifles with M1905 18-inch blade bayonets in M1910 scabbards, covered with OD webbing, are evident outside the humble quarters of Private Reinhardt of Company C, Sixteenth Infantry, at El Valle, Mexico, in September 1916. These long-edged weapons with walnut grips were seldom used, but nonetheless were an integral part of an infantryman's kit of the period. *NA*

Opposite page, lower left: Young Private Cronin of Company K, Sixteenth U.S. Infantry, has obtained a bold bandana as a non-regulation but practical addition to his Punitive Expedition uniform. His web belt, which had recently replaced the earlier russet belt, is worn with OD breeches. *NA*

Opposite page, lower right: A cook with the Sixteenth U.S. Infantry's second battalion, in his blue denim overalls, rolled brim 'Montana peak' and bandana, looks more like a cowpuncher than a foot soldier with Uncle Sam. He even seems to have pressed a pair of regulation cavalry gauntlets into service as 'hot pads' for his culinary duties on the Mexican border in 1916. *NA*

Left: In March 1916, while pursuing Pancho Villa into Mexico, men from Company B, Sixteenth U.S. Infantry, huddle against shelter halves that they have erected as partial windbreaks against the cold which was uncomfortable even at midday. Many are wearing the 1911-pattern olive drab sweater, including the battalion sergeant major on the right. *NA*

Left: When the United States entered World War I in 1917, shoulder sleeve insignia were adopted for divisions, corps, and armies, as well as certain other units. Once the Yanks arrived in Europe, the many changes to uniform included a British-type steel helmet, an 'overseas' cap after both French and English fashion, spiral puttees (wool leg wraps), and bronze disks with the company letter appearing below the crossed rifles and the regiment's number on the 'U.S.' disk (for ease of manufacture). Enlisted insignia of rank was to appear on the right sleeve only, above the elbow, as another wartime economy measure; previously, NCOs had worn chevrons on both sleeves. This 'doughboy', posing in Southampton, England, in October 1918, illustrates many of these particulars, along with the M1910 infantry equipment and M1918 hobnail boots. *NA*

Right: The first twelve divisions of 'doughboys' arriving in France were issued French-made light machine guns, while the next eleven divisions obtained .30 caliber British weapons which the Yanks designated as the Mark 1 Vickers, as seen here. *NA*

Right: This image illustrates a rare instance where not only crew-served weapons were of foreign make, but so were helmets, equipment, and small arms. Here the regimental band leads members of the 369th Infantry (formerly the 15th New York, a National Guard unit mobilized for the war) in U.S. uniforms and French equipage. This unit was part of the Ninety-third Division, whose enlisted men were black. *NA*

Right: Second Lieutenant George Sherwood, 131st Infantry, Thirty-third Division, shows off his British Military Cross presented for heroic conduct at Chippily, France in August 1918. His coat is typical for World War I American officers, being of a finer grade cloth than enlisted versions. The collar insignia also remained the larger bronze crossed rifles and 'U.S.' device, essentially as they were adopted in 1903. *NA*

Left: The trench coat became a common sight for officers serving in the AEF (American Expeditionary Forces) during World War I, as these two field grade officers depict. This privately purchased item offered better protection against rain than the regulation wool overcoat. Officers of the combat arms had overseas caps piped in branch colors, light blue being the correct hue for infantry. *NA*

Left: 'Doughboys,' most of whom are in the 1917-pattern enlisted overcoat, learn to operate the 37mm gun that was issued three per infantry regiment during the war. *NA*

Right: In this photograph, taken in October 1927, the .30 water-cooled Browning is pictured on a tripod as a light machine gun for use against enemy personnel. The crew serving this weapon wear the 1926-pattern olive drab coat with lapels, the upper ones now bearing not only the gilt or bright disks with the traditional crossed rifles on the left, below which appeared the company letter and the 'U.S.' device with regimental numeral on the right lapel, but also above them the distinctive unit insignia of the regiment. This was an extension of the practice of identifying a soldier's unit, introduced with World War I cloth shoulder sleeve insignia. *NA*

Left: Yanks in full battle regalia recreate 'going over the top' for the camera, just after the end of World War I. *NA*

Right: In this 1919 photograph, the First Brigade is being reviewed at Koblenz, Germany. Both officer and enlisted overcoats that were in use at the end of World War I are seen. The enlisted style is the 1918-pattern, which was shorter than its predecessor. Most of the officers in the center foreground have gold overseas stripes above their left cuffs, each indicating six months duty overseas, and many of them have also put aside the helmet for the 1912-pattern OD garrison hat with mohair band. *NA*

Right: Another post-World War I image, this time taken in 1921, of Company B, Eighth U.S. Infantry, a unit serving in Germany on occupation duty. They have put aside the overseas cap or helmet for inspection. All have the 1912-pattern enlisted garrison hat with large bronze disk insignia on the front of the model, as adopted in 1917 for enlisted men, as well as a special backing behind their collar insignia. The shoulder sleeve insignia of the Third Army is also prominent. For the most part, though, this is the basic World War I uniform, slightly smartened up. *NA*

Opposite page: Another change after World War I was the backing for chevrons, which after 1920 were cut out of OD cloth applied to a dark blue background. This change is evident on the sergeant standing to the left in the World War I type overseas cap and M1910 infantry equipment. Also evident is a grenade vest at the waist supported by means of a neck strap and a bandoleer for extra BAR (Browning automatic rifle) magazines. The soldier on the right wears the newly adopted 1926-pattern OD enlisted coat with open collar. Although this was a combat uniform, a black tie was to be worn with the olive drab pullover shirt, as shown by

this official 'before and after' photograph from 9 March 1927. *NA*

Above left and right: Side and rear view of the trio of photographs taken on 9 March 1927 captioned 'Old and New Soldier's Field Pack Infantry.' The sergeant on the left has a protective cover over this Springfield rifle and the private on the right wears a M1923 ammunition belt. *NA*

Below: The wheeled M1 mount could be hooked to a mule-drawn ammunition carrier for quick relocation. *NA*

Above: In this October 1927 photograph, an infantry crew aims at a mock target with a .30 caliber Browning water-cooled machine gun in the anti-aircraft position on a light wheeled M1 mount. *NA*

Left: This 1933 picture of the Twenty-fifth U.S. Infantry's color guard illustrates the widespread issue of the 1926-pattern coat and the version of the garrison cap adopted during at the same time as the basic garrison and field uniform. In 1934 a 'coat style' OD shirt began to replace the olive drab Oxford style pullover worn by these men, the former garment being open to the bottom and buttoning all the way down the front. *NA*

Right: Men of Company F, Twenty-fifth U.S. Infantry line up for chow in the 1934-pattern coat style OD coat style shirt without the black tie and M1938 dismounted leggings which had replaced the World War I wrap puttees. By this time (May 1942) the overseas cap had taken on a different look from its World War I predecessor, and trousers had replaced the breeches, a trend that started in 1938. Cotton khaki versions of this uniform also began to be issued late in the 1930s. *NA*

Above: Two men from the First Filipino Infantry Battalion train with the .30 caliber Browning water-cooled machine gun in April 1942. Their basic outfit, including the M1917A1 flat helmet, and the 'olive drab field jacket' specification PQD No. 20 (commonly referred to by collectors as the M1941 field jacket), and 1938-pattern OD wool trousers bloused into the M1938 dismounted leggings, was typical of the combat gear issued to first U.S. forces deployed early in World War II. Their instructor is a first sergeant, as indicated by his OD stripes on a dark blue background with the diamond above two arcs (changed to three arcs later in 1942). The light blue piping on his overseas cap was an addition to enlisted versions that did not exist during World War I, but made it possible to identify the wearer's branch of service, much like the piping on the 1902-pattern full dress enlisted uniform coat. *NA*

Opposite page, top: Men of Company C, 127th Infantry Regiment, 32nd Division, rest after capturing a Japanese position at Buna Mission, New Guinea. Besides the varied enemy souvenirs evident, the M1 helmet that became the trademark of World War II G.I.s is prominent. The helmet in the foreground rests on its top, showing some of the separate insert fiber liner that was an important feature of this protective headgear when it first began to be issued in earnest during 1942. *SC*

Opposite page, bottom: Two other members of the 127th Infantry Regiment in New Guinea have been issued the two-piece herringbone twill (HBT) fatigues that became common combat fare for summer (jungle/desert). They also wear the matching HBT hat (the prescribed shade was olive drab No. 7, although there are instances where a darker overdye was used) instead of the steel helmet. Both men have slung on fabric bandoleers to provide an extra forty-eight rounds for their rifles, in addition to the eighty rounds carried in their M1923 ammunition belts. The man on the left holds an M1910 aluminum canteen. *SC*

Right: Heavily laden with their M1928 haversacks, men of the 148th Infantry Regiment, 37th Division, go over the side of their transports to participate in the late 1943 invasion of Bougainville. All seem to have discarded their awkward leggings, a practice that many infantrymen followed in the Pacific Theater. The man nearest the bottom of the net has an 1903 Springfield bolt-action rifle, one being issued per squad to act as a grenade launcher prior to development of the M1 rifle to serve this purpose. *SC*

Opposite page, top: Enjoying their Christmas day repast in Italy during 1943, three men with the 3d Infantry Division use the typical field mess kit issued to troops in all theaters during the war. The man on the right not only wears the division shoulder sleeve insignia on his field jacket, but also has it painted on his M1 helmet, a matter more of individual taste than standard practice – although not uncommon. *SC*

Opposite page, bottom: In late July 1944, Private John Bender goes into action with his 2.4-inch rocket launcher, better known as a 'bazooka,' against Japanese holding out in a cave on Saipin. This thirteen-pound weapon was provided to infantry units to bolster firepower. It fired both anti-personnel and anti-tank projectiles, and was equipped with a battery-operated electronic firing mechanism. *SC*

Top right: Mud and snow were powerful enemies of the World War II foot soldier. The M1944 12-inch shoe pac lined with rubber, and featuring a leather top that laced high up on the leg, was one ally in defeating this twin hazard. A pair of these protective items is being worn by the man in the foreground, who is a member of the 34th Infantry Division serving in Italy during November 1944. *SC*

Right: Most of the members of the 423rd Infantry Regiment's Intelligence and Reconnaissance Platoon seen here at St Vith, Belgium on 16 December 1944 are wearing the M1943 olive drab field jacket. This outer garment was designed to be windproof and water repellent and was issued in both temperate and cold climates. It also had four large pockets that could be crammed with all sorts of necessities in the field, and could be combined with a detachable hood. Four of the group have cloth helmet nets that could be used to affix foliage for camouflage, or at least to reduce glare from the sun striking the body of the helmet. *SC*

Right: General Mark Clark, commanding the Fifth U.S. Army in Italy, presents battle streamers on 16 November 1944 to guidon bearers of the 168th Infantry Regiment, 34th Division, in their 'smartened up' versions of the M1943 field uniform. The guidons are medium blue with white. *SC*

Above: Men of the 71st Infantry Regiment, 44th Division reach the shore after crossing the River Danube, near Berg, Germany, on 23 April 1945. One of the first members of the squad off the barge carries the famous M1918A1 BAR, a .30 caliber gas-operated, air-cooled weapon that combined rifle and machine gun capabilities to enhance the U.S. foot infantry's firepower at the basic unit level. The cloth helmet covers seen here were not typically worn in the field. *SC*

Right: A member of the highly decorated 442nd Regimental Combat team is identified by his Statue of Liberty torch shoulder sleeve insignia, commonly called a patch. Men of this unit were Japanese Americans who fought in the European Theater with great valor. Here, the young G.I. goes through the papers of a captured German NCO. He wears the two-buckle boot with 5-inch leather cuff that was tested in North Africa in 1943 and issued in fairly substantial quantities during the last two years of the war, gradually eliminating the need for leggings. *SC*

INDEX